Acadia National Park
Animals & Attractions

Billy Grinslott & Kinsey Marie Books

ISBN - 9781960612915

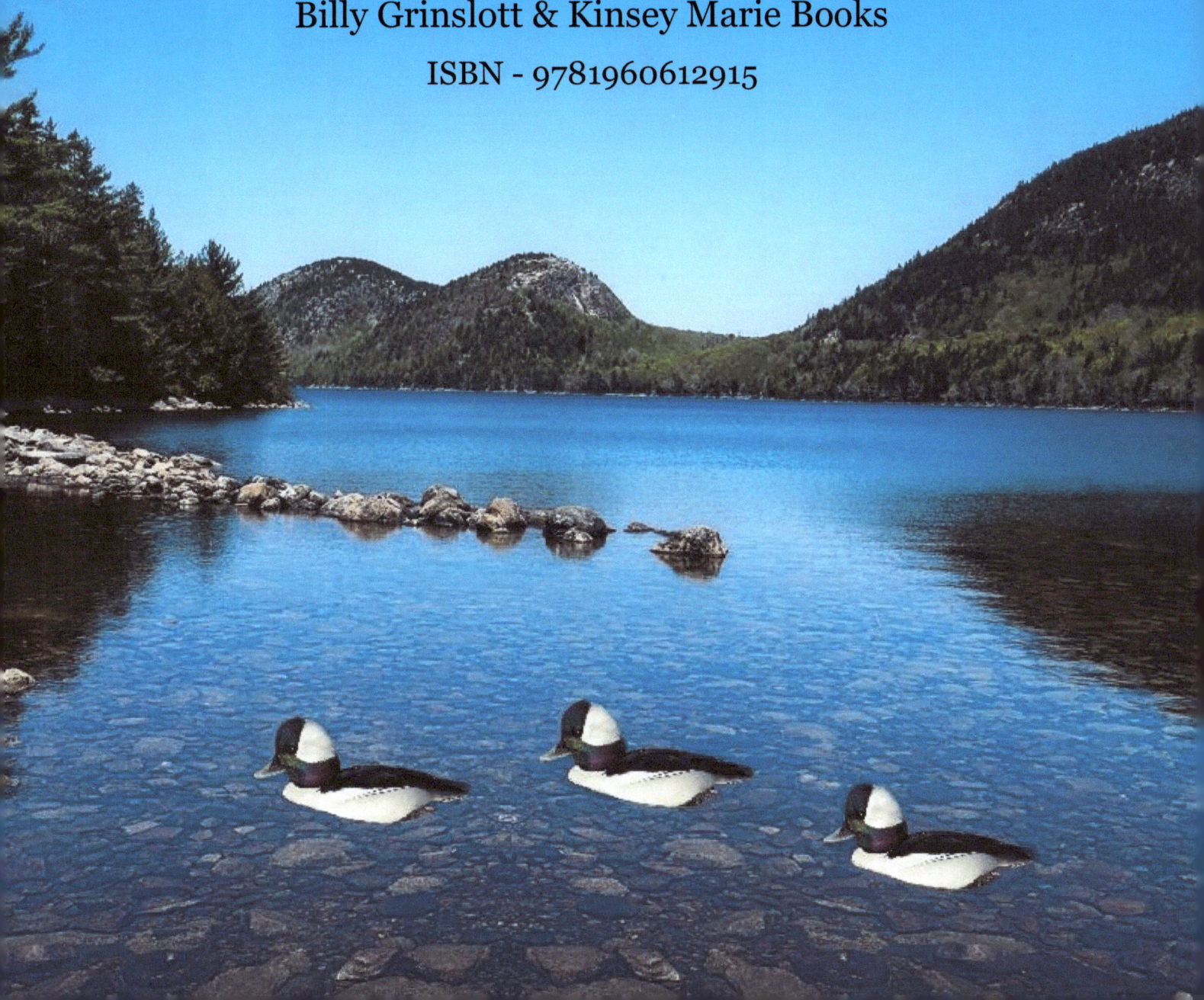

There are many animals in Acadia. We have listed the more popular ones that would be fun to see while hiking.

There are many squirrels in the wild. You may see a red or gray squirrel. The most popular is the gray squirrel. Squirrels are very acrobatic and can climb trees. Their favorite food is acorns. They like to collect acorns and eat them later.

The hare is bigger than a rabbit with longer ears and legs. Their longs legs help them to run fast. They are agile and faster than most rabbits. Hares have excellent hearing and vision. Hares have large ears and eyes that are positioned on the sides of their head, giving them a wide field of vision. Hares can change color. Hares have the ability to change color depending on the season and their surroundings.

The American Mink lives across most of North America and is a cat sized. Mink are very skilled climbers and swimmers. They prefer to keep to themselves. They communicate using odors, visual signals, and other sounds. They purr when they're happy. Mink are agile swimmers, and they often dive to find food.

Otters have the thickest fur of any animal. The otter is one of the few mammals that use tools. A group of otters resting together is called a raft.

Otters primarily rely on their sense of touch, whiskers, and forepaws, in murky waters to locate food. Otters have built in pouches of loose skin under their forearms to stash extra food when diving.

Fishers are native to North America. They hiss and growl when upset. They are closely related to badgers, mink, and otters. Fisher young are known as kits. Fishers are one of the few animals that eat porcupines. Fishers are also called pekan, pequam, wejack, and woolang.

Martens can be distinguished from fishers, because martens are smaller, have orange on their throats and chests, and have pointier ears and snouts. Martens are part of the weasel family. They are very rare and hard to find. Their tail is long, about two thirds of their body size. There are 13 subspecies of American marten that are native to North America.

Beavers use their teeth to cut and knock down trees. They build dams with them to block water, so they have a place to live and swim. They also eat wood. Beavers can stay underwater for about 8 minutes. Beavers slap their tails on the water to indicate danger. Beavers are the largest rodents in North America.

Porcupines have sharp quills on their backs to help protect them. A porcupine can have up to 30 thousand quills, they are sharp and will stick you if you touch them. To communicate they make grunts and high-pitched noises. A group of porcupines is called a family.

Raccoons like to come out at night. Their eyes are made so they can see in the dark. They are called masked bandits because they have a dark mask around their eyes, and they like to raid and eat out of trash cans at night.

Bobcats are frequently misidentified as a lynx. Bobcats are part of the lynx family, but they are smaller than a lynx with different markings.

There are several types of foxes in North America. This is a red fox. Females are called vixens. Red foxes have supersonic hearing. When afraid, red foxes grin or look like they are smiling. Red foxes front paws have five toes, while their hind feet only have four. There are red and gray foxes in the national park.

The coyote is bigger than a fox. Eastern coyotes are part wolf. Coyotes are great for pest control. They like to eat mice and rats. They can adapt and live almost anywhere, even in the city. They have a yip type of call when they communicate with each other. Coyotes are found in all the United States, except Hawaii.

The whitetail deer is the most popular deer in North America. Whitetail deer have good eyesight and hearing. Only male deer grow antlers, which are shed each year. Whitetail deer are good swimmers and will use large streams and lakes to escape predators. A young deer is called a fawn. They are the most common deer species and live everywhere in North America.

There are six different subspecies of moose found in the forests. Moose are built for cold areas and like living in cold regions. Moose are huge and weigh up to 800 pounds. Moose love water and are good swimmers. Moose are part of the deer family. At 5 days old they can outrun a person. As very large mammals that need a great deal of space, moose are rarely seen in Acadia.

Black bears are the smallest members of the bear family in North America. Black Bears love to eat sweet things like berries, fruits, and vegetables. They are good climbers and fast runners. They usually sleep for long periods of time and hibernate during the winter. They typically try to stay away from people. Black bears are rarely seen in Acadia but there is a permanent year-round population on Mount Desert Island.

If you do some sightseeing near the ocean, you will probably see some of these next few animals. Seals and sea lions. The smallest seal species is the Galapagos Fur Seal the largest is the elephant seal. Seals can sleep underwater. Seals can dive up to 2000 feet. Seals can be hooligans. They like to have fun and are very friendly. Mother seals and pups, bond with a unique call. Their brain temperature drops when they dive, to protect their brain.

Dolphins and porpoises can be found all over the world. There are 36 species of dolphins, living in nearly all aquatic environments. Dolphins are usually slow swimmers, travelling at about 2 mph. But they can reach speeds of over 30 mph for brief periods. When trying to capture food, dolphins produce bubbles to herd their prey to the surface. Dolphins are usually very friendly. But it doesn't mean you should approach them.

Humpback Whales. Visiting in spring and summer, these acrobatic giants are known for their breaching and tail-slapping behavior. Other whales you might see are Minke, Orca Killer Whales, Beluga, Pilot, Finback, Right, and Bar Harbor whales. They are fun to watch as they breech the surface of the water. Whales communicate by singing to each other. They are cool to listen too.

There are many sights to see at Acadia national park. We've listed some of the more popular ones. Most of the ones we listed will take you to other areas. If you want to see more sights without the animals, check out our Acadia National Parks attractions and sights to see book.

Park Loop Road is one of the best ways to drive through Acadia national park. The Park Loop Road is one of three types of major road systems in Acadia. This 27-mile road is the go-to scenic drive. It connects Acadia's lakes, mountains, and shoreline. It provides access to popular areas in the park.

Ocean Path. Explore vast slabs of pink granite, cliffs, and oceans views. The Ocean Path takes you along the coast of Maine. The Ocean Path is a great way to access Thunder Hole and Otter Point from Sand Beach on a gradual hike. Hiking Distance is 2.2 miles one way, or 4.4 miles round trip.

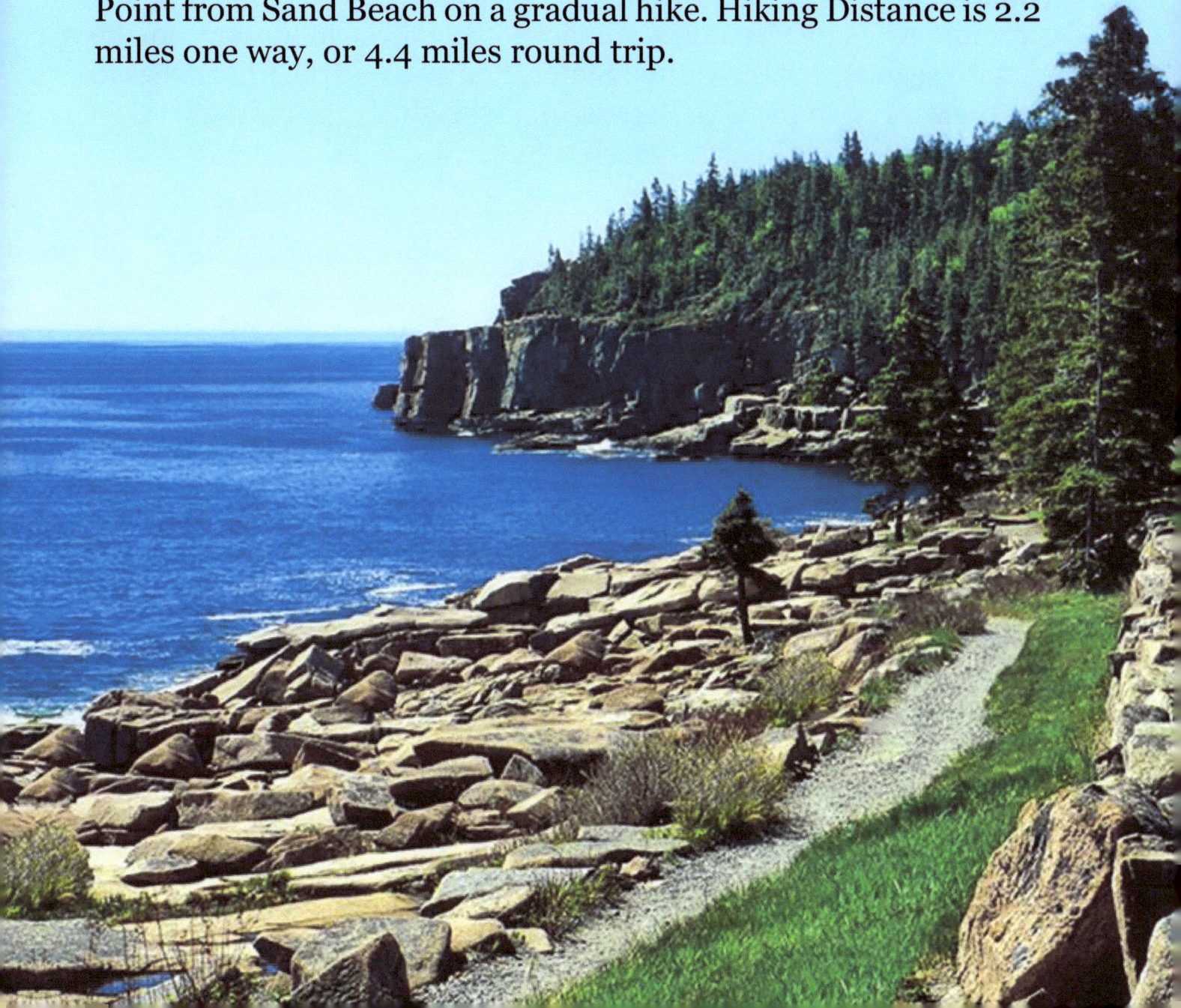

Cadillac Mountain is a popular destination for visitors. It is accessible by car. It offers magnificent views of a glacier coastal and island landscape areas. The short, paved Cadillac Summit Loop Trail connects to waysides, restrooms, and a gift shop is located at the summit. At 1530 feet tall, Cadillac is the tallest mountain on the eastern seaboard of the United States. It is also one the first places to see the sunrise in the U.S. Because of its height.

Jordan Pond is one of the park's most pristine lakes, with awesome surrounding mountain scenery. Glaciers carved the landscape, leaving behind numerous features. Jordan Pond has multitudes of visitors who enjoy canoeing and kayaking. Jordan Pond path, 3.3-mile loop has forested areas with uneven footing on wooden boardwalks, rocks, and footbridges.

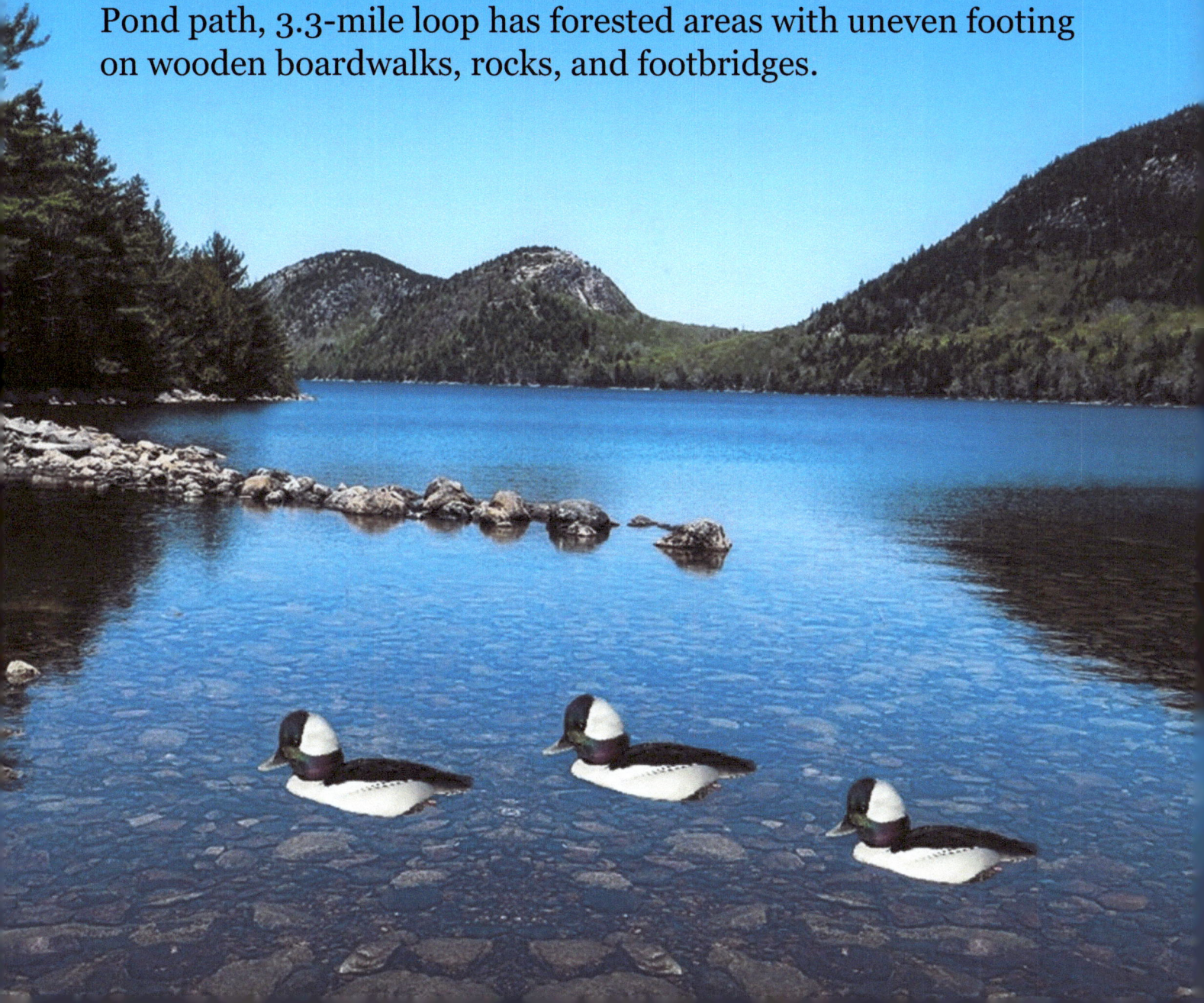

The Schoodic Peninsula is the only part of Acadia found on the mainland. The 6 mile one-way loop road around Schoodic Peninsula offers views of lighthouses, seabirds, and forested islands. Use turnouts to stop and enjoy the scenery. Enjoy riding the Schoodic Loop Road and the 8.3 miles of bike paths. Steep and winding bike paths provide spectacular views.

Carraige Roads has 45 miles of roads to enjoy, but not by car. Pedestrians, bicyclists, horses, and horse-drawn carriages share in the access, and safety of these auto-free roads across the park. The roads were built to preserve the scenic views of the park without the use of motorized vehicles. The views and scenery are spectacular.

This hike on Great Head Trail is an awesome mix of ocean views, rocky scrambles, and hidden history of Acadia. Near the top of the granite steps of the hike, is a large millstone dating back to the 1900's. The ruins of stone tower, built in the 1900's still remain there today. The trail is rocky with uneven footing, good footwear is recommended. Hiking distance is 1.9 miles round trip.

Thunder Hole. If you want to get wet, this is the place to visit. When the waves are right, the water rushes into thunder hole and gushes up into the air. Spraying everything around it. Be careful not to walk on the platform if the waves are bad, because they may wash you off the platform. Best to use caution when visiting this area.

Sieur de Monts, often referred to as the Heart of Acadia. Includes Sieur de Monts Spring and spring house, A Nature Center, the Wild Gardens of Acadia, the tarn, the Great Meadow Wetland, and access to multiple historic memorial paths. It is the first major stopping point along the Park Loop Road. It's a great way to see the beauty of the park. There are multiple different paths to take, depending on what parts of the park you want to see.

The Bass Harbor Head Light Station it is located in Tremont, Maine, marking the entrance to Bass Harbor and Blue Hill Bay. There are about 80 lighthouses across Maine, this is one of three lights managed by Acadia National Park. With 180,000 annual visitors, the light station is the most visited place on the west side of Mount Desert Island. It was constructed in 1858.

Bubble Rock is composed of Lucerne Granite. Lucerne Granite did not form on Mount Desert Island in Acadia. It formed 30 miles northwest of Acadia. How did a 100-ton boulder move such a distance? Bubble Rock was carried by a glacier and deposited in a different area inside Acadia national park. There are 2 large rocks that made this journey during the ice age and bubble rock is one of them. The hiking distance to see bubble rock is 1.6 miles roundtrip.

Sand Beach is a popular summertime destination on Park Loop Road. Surrounded by cliffs, this small stretch of coast is the largest sandy beach in Acadia. Relax by the waves, take a swim, or head out on a nearby trail and enjoy this area. Ocean Path, Beehive Loop, and Gorham Mountain Loop can all be accessed here. You can drive to sand beach or take a free shuttle bus.

Otter Cliff or Otter Point is one of the most spectacular sights along the North Atlantic Seaboard. On the east side of the Park Loop Road is the 110-foot-high Otter cliff. One of the highest Atlantic coastal areas north of Rio de Janeiro. Just before Otter Cliff is a spot called Monument Cove. Right after this, the road begins to curve to the left. To the right is a small parking area. On the other side of the street is a path that leads to otter cliff. It has spectacular views of the surrounding area.

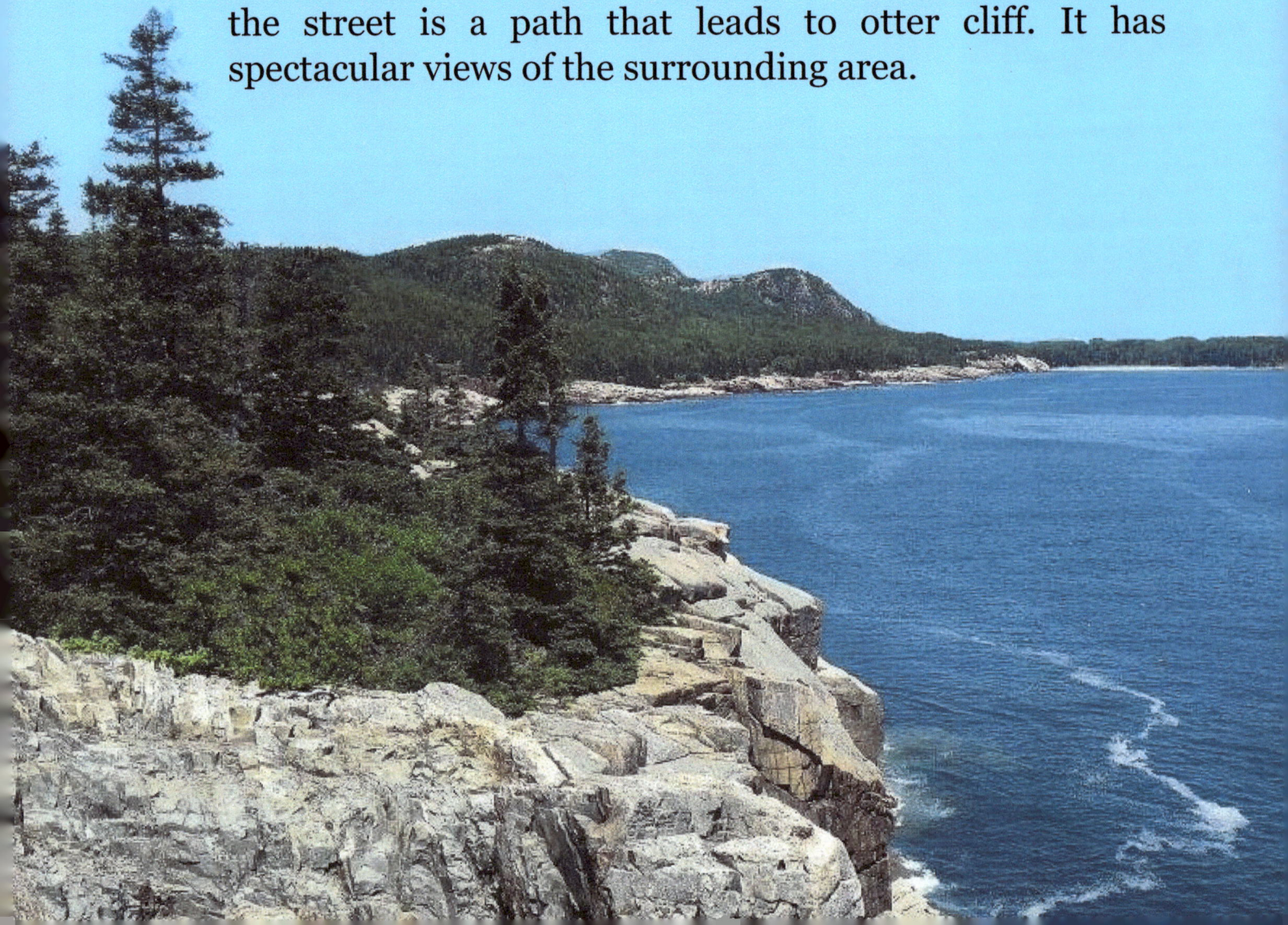

Precipice Trail is not for most people. The trail is narrow and involves climbing steep areas. Rising over 1,000 feet in 0.9 miles, the trail requires physical and mental strength. It is a rugged, non-technical climb with open cliff faces and iron rungs. If you make it to the summit, awesome views are awarded.

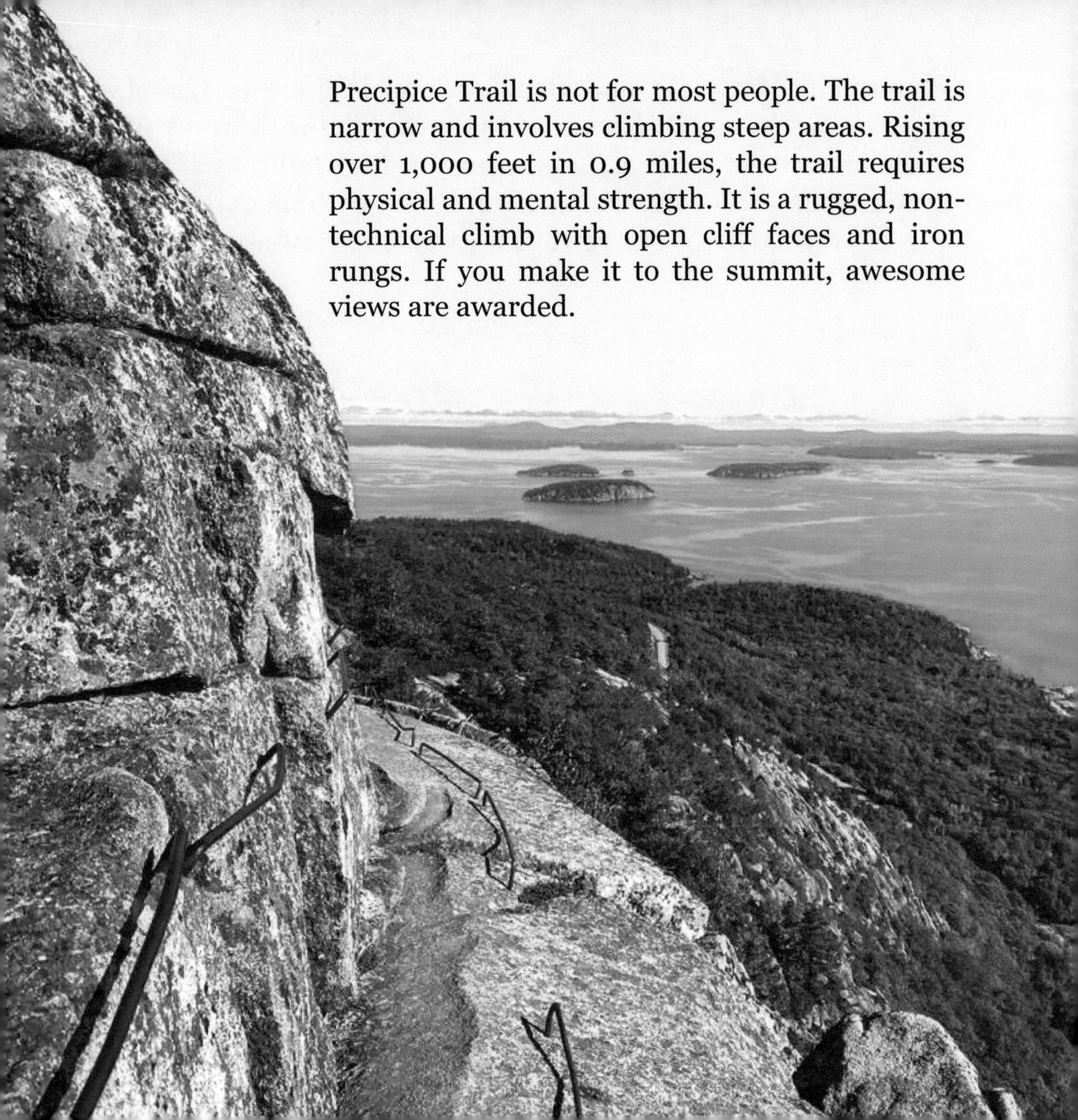

Champlain Mountain and Beehive loop is another trail for experienced hikers. It has areas that are steep with iron rungs to hang onto. In general, conditions on the trail may include muddy areas, steep climbs, and wet rocks, with huge boulders. It is a 6.6-mile loop. The reward is awesome views.

Gorham Mountain Loop provides an excellent overview of what Acadia has to offer. Rocky coastline, Cadillac Mountain in the distance, and a panoramic view of the ocean await those who hikes this loop trail. Head out on this 3.0-mile loop trail, considered a moderately challenging route. It is a beautiful and well-marked trail with multiple scenic views perfect for taking pictures.

Beech Mountain Trail is a short, moderate loop on the west side of Mount Desert Island, Beech Mountain Trail provides hikers with views of Long Pond and Mansell Mountain and access to one of the few remaining fire towers in the area. This hike is also a good sunset with great views. Hiking distance is 1.2 miles round trip. The Terrain is a forested path, with rocky trails, granite stairs and slopes, wooden steps.

Echo Lake is a popular spot for swimming, kayaking, and fishing, and offers stunning views of the surrounding mountains. Echo Beach is a rather small beach in a cove surrounded by cliffs and trees. Lifeguards are usually on duty. It is quite pretty and worth a visit. It is accessible off Route 102 in Southwest Harbor.

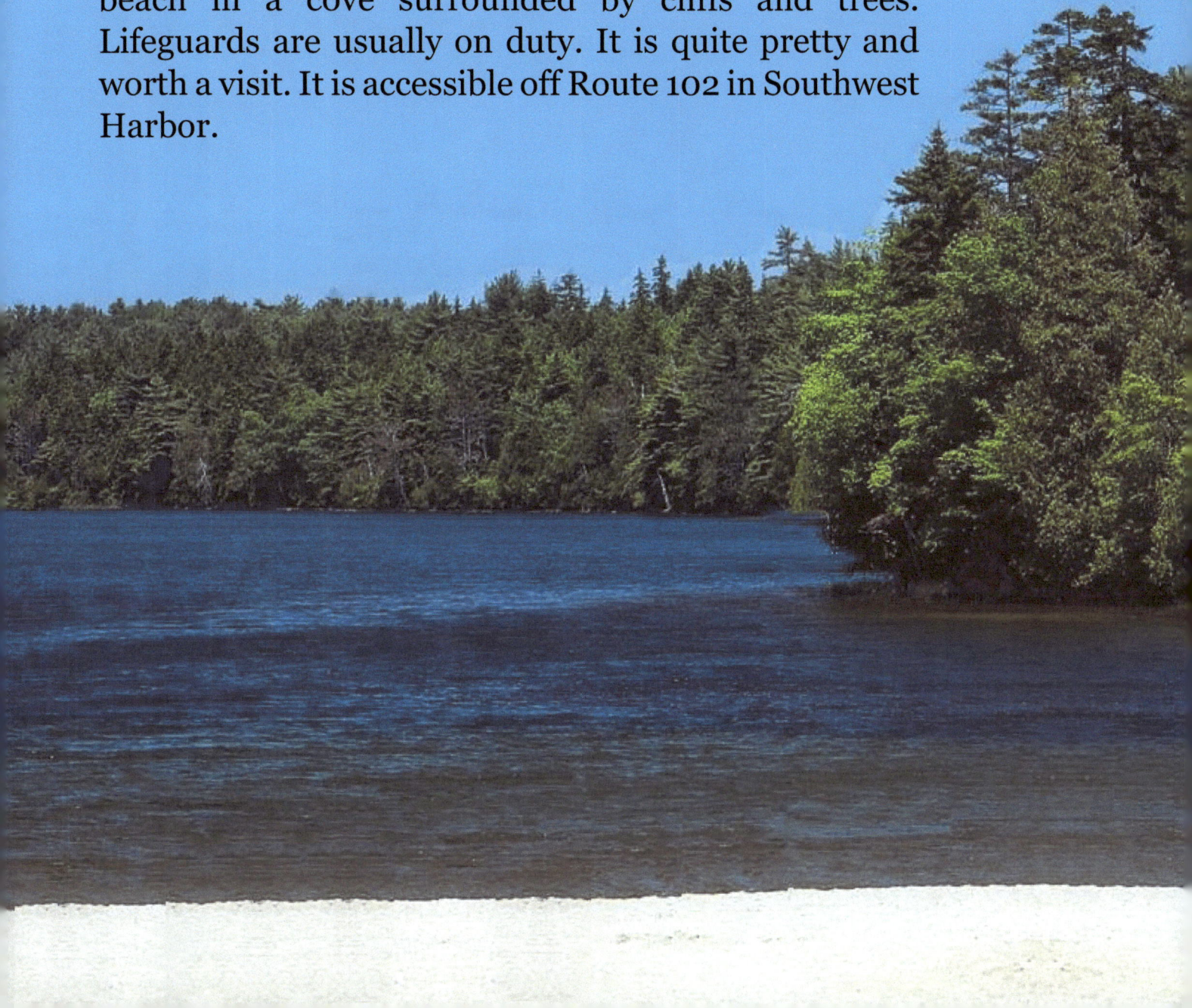

The Dorr Mountain South Ridge Loop features panoramic views of Mount Desert Island from the top of Dorr Mountain. It has a strenuous beginning climb with a long descent through the forest. Dorr Mountain has lots of boulder scrambling over steep grades. The view from the top is wonderful, but you'll have to work hard to get there. Distance is 3.2 miles round trip.

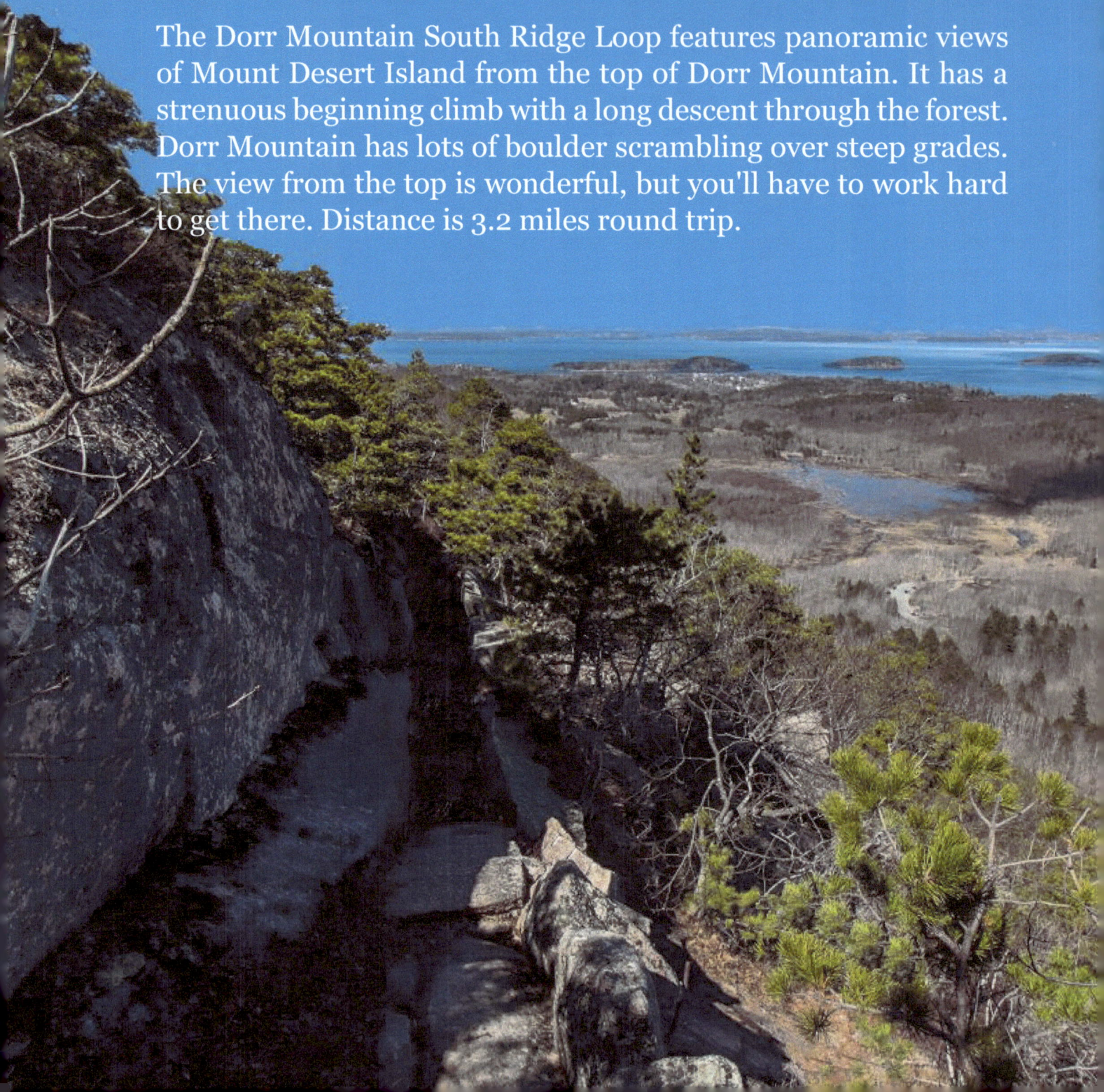

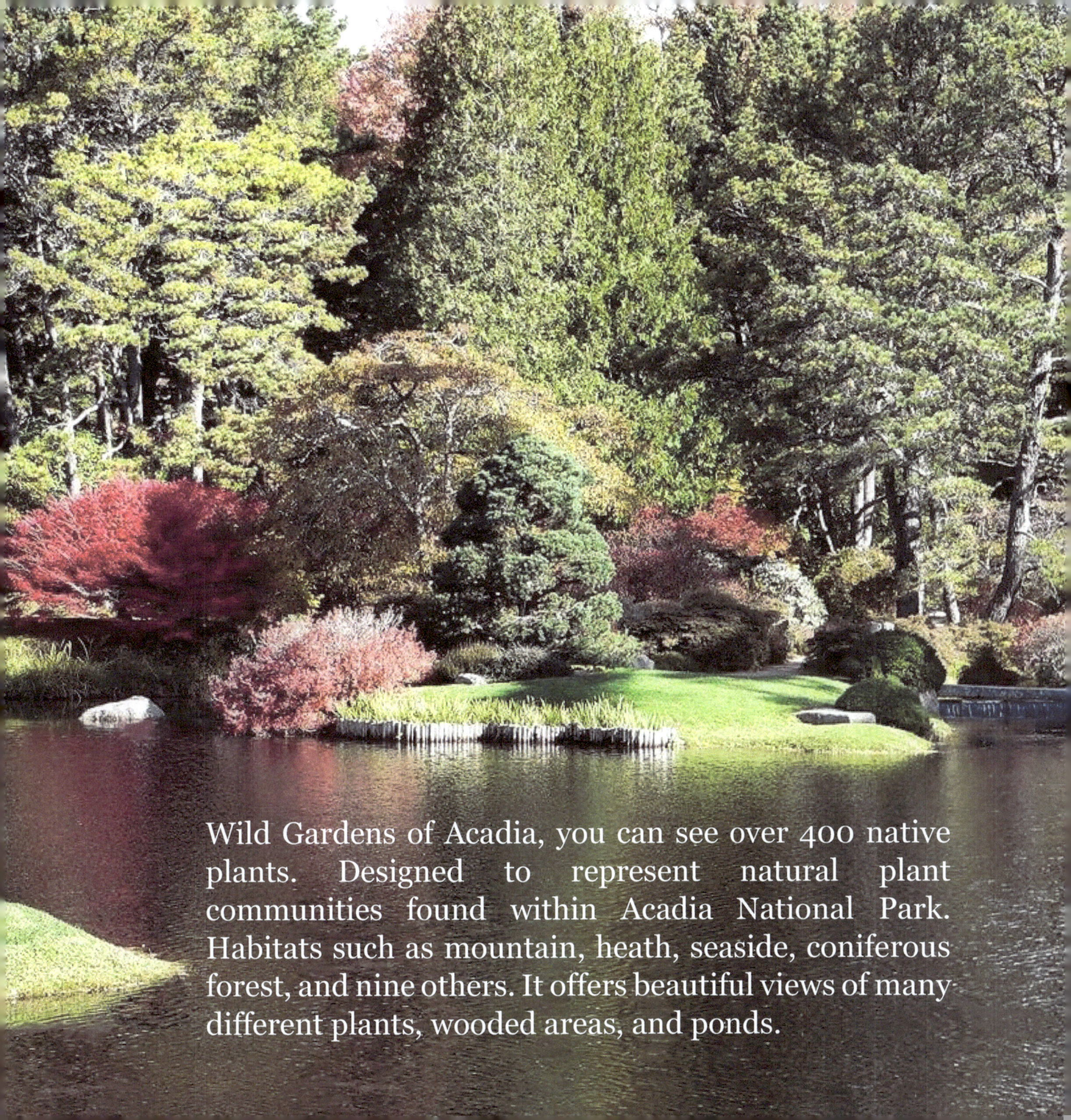

Wild Gardens of Acadia, you can see over 400 native plants. Designed to represent natural plant communities found within Acadia National Park. Habitats such as mountain, heath, seaside, coniferous forest, and nine others. It offers beautiful views of many different plants, wooded areas, and ponds.

1. Acadia National Park was established on February 26, 1919, it is the oldest designated national park east of the Mississippi River.

2. Acadia is open year-round, however some of the areas in the park are closed from October through late May. Bird watchers come from all over the world in the hopes of viewing. The many different birds that visit Acadia national park.

3. The park has 26 mountains, including the tallest peak along the North Atlantic Seaboard, Cadillac Mountain at 1530 feet high.

4. In 2016 Acadia National Park had almost 3.5 million visitors, making it one of the most popular parks in the National Park Service.

5. There are many ways to enjoy the park. You can hike it, bike it or drive to many sightseeing spots. They have guided tour vehicles, or you can take carriages with horses, or you can ride a horse.

6. You can even take a boat ride or kayak on some of the lakes. They have swimming areas, camping areas, and you can fish.

7. Always make plans before going to Acadia. Some areas require permits or reservations. Plan before going.

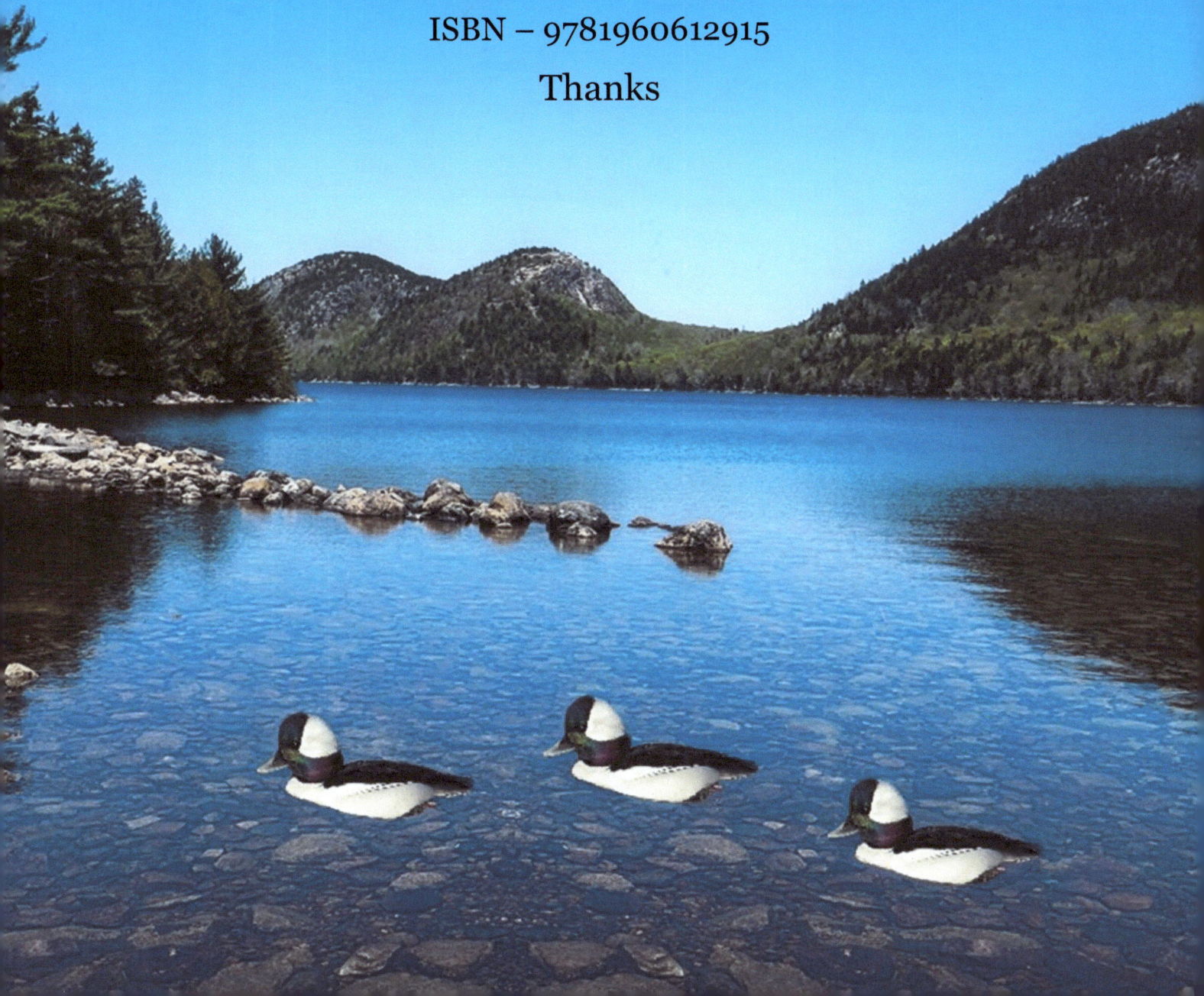

Author Page

Billy Grinslott & Kinsey Marie Books

Copyright, All Rights Reserved

ISBN – 9781960612915

Thanks